CHINESE BUSINESS DINNER CULTURE:

Mistakes to Avoid and Critical Must Do's to Gain Face, Impress Decision Makers and Close More Deals

By Dr. Justin Trosclair, D.C.

Edited by: Dr. Emer Garry

Copyright © 2019 Text by Dr. Justin Trosclair, D.C.

Dedication

To my wife, Jing Jing. She is by far one of the most supportive people I know. She has been a constant encouragement when I explore new ideas and she flexes my creative side. From starting a weekly interview-based podcast over three years ago (www.adoctorsperspective.net), writing several books, traveling, raising a daughter and brainstorming new ideas, you listen, challenge me, and make me a better person.

To the owner of the hospital I worked at for nearly five years, Mr. Li. Thank you for being such an advocate for chiropractic care in a country where there are no schools or official licenses. We both took a risk in collaborating but it's been of mutual benefit. I've enjoyed my time sharing dinners with co-workers and big deals who came to town. You play a large part in how I quickly learned the do's and don'ts of creating a successful business dinner.

Exclusive Access

As a special thank you for buying this book, you have unique access to videos to see select areas of the book in action. To gain access to the videos, please contact me at drtrosclair@gmail.com or visit www.drjustintrosclair.com to find the contact form and the latest social media updates. I look forward to hearing from you and if you need any personal assistance or coaching in this topic or health, reach out and connect with me.

Disclaimer

This book is meant to provide general information and guidance about another culture's corporate dinner etiquette. It should not be used as sole guidance for making any business decisions. The content is not written as personal advice. Results and closing more business deals are not guaranteed. This work is provided without express or limited warranty of any kind by either the author or anyone who has been involved in the creation, production, or distribution of this book. This includes, but is not limited to, the implied warranties of business advice for a particular purpose. The determination of the risk and usability of the information contained herein rests entirely with the reader. Justin Trosclair, editors, and the final publisher of this book recommend that you seek a qualified and experienced professional when implementing any type of advice on making sales and corporate decisions for your business, whether conducted locally, internationally, or in China. The publisher and author assume no responsibility, warranties, or guarantees of any kind for any errors or omissions. In no case shall the author be held responsible for any loss or other damages caused by the use and misuse of, or inability to use, any or all of the information described in this book. The information within this book represents the views of the author at the date of publication. Due to the rapid increase in knowledge and cultural changes, the author reserves the right to update and modernize his views at any time. While every attempt has been made to verify the information, the author cannot accept responsibility for inaccuracies or oversights. Any perceived disrespect against organizations or individual persons is unintentional. The author makes no guarantee or warranty about the reader's success when using this material. You agree to these terms by taking legal possession of this document. If this agreement is violated, you will be notified via certified mail to cease the use of this campaign. You will lose your lifetime right to implement this material for your personal use.

Reproduction of Material

This book should not be reprinted, emailed, faxed, sold, copied, or distributed to others in any way. Consider the information in this book as copyrighted just like any book you would buy. Digital and print books have the same legal rights. Please don't commit illegal sharing. Even if you received this book free from a promotion, you paid for it by exchanging a valid email address. I expect the same from other readers. Thank you for being honest.

Please respect the effort it takes to write a book of any caliber and don't email or print this for others. What you can do is share the website www.adoctorperspective.net or www.drjustintrosclair.com and look for the book link. You can also go to online book stores to purchase this book.

About the Author

Dr. Justin Trosclair is a practicing chiropractic doctor and obtained his degree from the Texas Chiropractic College in Pasadena, TX with academic honors. He was born and raised in the heart of Cajun Country, Louisiana and received a Bachelor of Science from Louisiana State University. Dr. Justin spent almost seven years practicing in a suburb of Denver, Colorado before working at a hospital in Yunnan, China for five years. Dr. Trosclair is also the host of "A Doctor's Perspective" podcast where he interviews doctors about their specialties, marketing, staff concerns, overcoming obstacles, entertainment and maintaining a thriving and loving family life. Please visit www.adoctorsperspective.net to listen and why not subscribe so you never miss an episode or other announcements. His clinic website can be found at www.drjustintrosclair.com. Dr. Justin is happily married to an amazing woman and they have one daughter. He can't say enough good things about JJ and would feel remiss if he left any out. Dr. Trosclair is available for interviews, guest speaking, personal coaching, and many other opportunities. He can be contacted at drtrosclair@gmail.com.

REVIEWS

I heed his motto, "Observe what they are doing and mimic." Patiently waiting for where to sit and for the good dishes to come my way is just one way this book helped me and a few colleagues to feel more comfortable with an unfamiliar culture. The few Chinese words I learned made them smile, clap and toast more at dinner. I was happy to not offend anyone and no one lost face. They had nothing but nice things to say about us, at least that's what the translator told us.

Vaughn T. - Petroleum and Gas Industry, USA

One of the things that stood out for me was the toasts (and sometimes shots). Tapping the table instead of raising your glass was surprising. I'm glad I found that out before attending the dinners. I felt like a local and less like a newbie.

Hope C. - Corrections Officer, USA

I went to a wedding in China and came across this book. The videos you made helped me to know the best words to learn, counting, and the examples of dinner etiquette were excellent. Locals appreciated our effort to honor their customs and traditions. You helped make our trip so much easier and our confidence to interact with family was much higher knowing how to use body language along with the translator.

Debbie T. - Tourist for a Wedding, USA

I was fortunate enough to come across Justin's advice halfway into my consulting month in Shanghai. I learned a few things by watching others at dinner. but it was the smaller details that I learned from him that made all the difference. Now I understood why people sat where they did, what order to toast, and how dinners could impact how seriously they took my proposals. PS: I got an amazing reference letter at the end.

Niclas B. - Financial Project Manager, Germany

My experience in China was the most life-changing adventure. Spending time with local people and learning all of their customs was fun with the guidance of Justin Trosclair. He helped me prepare for my trip, but seeing it in real life still shocked me a little. Some of those things were eating etiquettes: If you don't like a piece of meat, you just spit it on the ground. They eat the WHOLE animal (nothing is boneless in China), and you rarely turn down an alcoholic drink offer. Besides that, they are pretty much like any typical family. They always want to feed you, make sure you have everything you need, and a smile goes a long way. Make sure you bring your tissue paper because there isn't usually any in the bathrooms. Yes, sometimes a toilet is indeed a squatty potty.

Ali D.B. - Manager Of Naturopathic Office
and Wedding Guest, USA

TABLE OF CONTENTS

Dedication i

Exclusive Access.. i

Disclaimer ii

Reproduction of Material....................................... iii

About the Author.. iv

Reviews.. v

Learn What to Do and What Not To Do at Dinner to Gain Face, Impress Decision Makers and Close More Deals 1

What is "Face" in Chinese Society? 3

Chapter One: Background...................................... 5

Chapter Two: Restaurant Layout 10

    Chopstick Protocol... 12

Chapter Three: Where to Sit and Beginning of Dinner 15

Chapter Four: Toasting, Drinking, and Smoking 21

    Toast Order... 22

    How to Hold the Cup 25

Dinner Buzz Words in Chinese 29

Your Toasting Phrases 30

Fake Drinking 31

Smoking 32

Chapter Five: Eating Etiquette 35

How to Hold Chopsticks 36

How Should I Serve Myself 38

How Much Food to Take 41

Where to Put the Bones and Other Waste 42

Food Topics 43

Dietary Restrictions 46

To Sum It Up 47

Bonus Chapter 49

The Tea Ceremony 49

Other Books by Dr. Justin Trosclair, D.C. 54

LEARN WHAT TO DO AND WHAT NOT TO DO AT DINNER TO GAIN FACE, IMPRESS DECISION MAKERS AND CLOSE MORE DEALS

You have decided to do business in China for many reasons. I'm not going to pretend to know everything about how to navigate Chinese businesspeople and how they differ from Western-based societies because you can find multiple books on that topic plus an entire university degree. I do know about business dinners and lunches that follow meetings with long tables, comfortable chairs, a slideshow presentation, and a portfolio bound together nicely.

A big piece of Chinese culture, particularly business culture, which is why you're reading this book, is these lunches and dinners. It's a completely different culture and no one would blame you for being confused, but I will guarantee that after reading this book, you are going to be well advanced in your business dinner etiquette for Chinese culture. You will be able to impress them and look amazing compared to their past dealings with foreigners.

You will be able to avoid the common mistakes that many people make that could undermine your credibility in their eyes. Chinese people talk about gaining and losing face and after finishing this short book, you can rest assured that gaining face is what you and your soon to be colleagues will experience. So trust the words that are written here based on my many experiences.

WHAT IS "FACE" IN CHINESE SOCIETY?

Gaining or losing face is extremely important in China. If you're reading this book that means you probably read another book discussing this aspect of their culture. As a Westerner, I look at the face concept as respect, pride, reputation or boosting your ego. If you can do or say something that can make the other person look competent, amazing, special, excel at their job and other similar scenarios, you are allowing them to gain face. If, however, you embarrass them, make them look foolish or incompetent, you're causing them to lose face. That means they look incompetent to their peers, co-workers, boss, etc., and nobody likes to look stupid. The difference is that this culture can go to extreme lengths to avoid losing face. Let's illustrate with the following example.

If you were to ask someone a question and they don't know the answer, they will not want to disappoint a foreigner, so they will say yes, even if they know they can't fulfill or do the task. When you ask someone to prepare a document, ask how something works, whether a task can be accomplished or if a document is translated correctly, the answer you may hear is yes. They might say what they think you want to hear, which may not be accurate. That's an aspect of saving face that becomes irritating to a foreigner.

If you are unaware of this tendency, you will be working with bad information or expect them to be able to do something they can't do. The major problem is that you won't know about it until later. Now you look silly because they were too embarrassed to say they couldn't do something just to save face. A deadline could pass or an incorrect product could be released because of this, which wastes time and money.

My tip: Read their body language when asking a question. They may break eye contact, fidget, or if you have a gut feeling then you should probably trust it. When I ask an important question and get that "strange vibe", I will ask it in a simpler way from a different angle, or in a way that allows them to say no and still save face while still getting a true answer. I know it would be easier if they were just honest upfront instead of losing even more face on the backend when they can't deliver on what they agreed. It's just one of those cultural differences we have to accept and find a workaround for.

> *Again, when you're asking questions and need results, sometimes you have to ask it a couple of different ways so they can say NO and not lose face.

Dinners have an element of flattering and talking to leaders, CEOs, the "big deals" and the influencers. Knowing who to give face to is a first key step in building the rapport you need to close the deal.

CHAPTER ONE:

BACKGROUND

Why do I feel qualified to write this book? Back in 2013, I sold my chiropractic clinic in Colorado to travel the world. I didn't want to spend all the money I made from the sale, but I was on a mission to find a place where I didn't have to retake boards, could do chiropractic work, and make enough money to travel and live comfortably. China fit all my criteria and after a few months of emails back and forth I found myself on my first 15-hour international flight.

I had 30,000 RMB (about USD 5,000 at the time) in a hidden money belt because I didn't know exactly what kind of apartment deposits I would need, what furniture to purchase, and how much living expenses would be for the first month with no paycheck. Little did I know that this much RMB was a year's salary for many of the nurses in that hospital.

The first week was a whirlwind of confusion. I had a translator who could barely understand my accent (and vice versa) and a new culture that I was grossly underprepared to navigate. As time went on, the translator and I learned how to communicate with each other better. I spoke at a slower cadence and used simpler words. Explaining a disc bulge and what an evidence-based chiropractor can do for it was not an easy task, but after a couple of months, my translator understood. We picked up on each other's slang, nuances of our languages, accents, and we became great friends for the rest of that year.

The first night we went to a hole in the wall restaurant that was not very clean and ordered some lose peanuts (no shell) and a couple of dishes. This was my first experience with communal dishes on a table and people double-dipping. All the bowls of food, whether it was green leafy vegetables, a pork dish, peanuts, etc. were placed in the middle of the table. I didn't dive into the food right away. I observed people using their chopsticks to grab a bite directly from the central bowls. Sometimes they put it in their own bowl that was already filled with rice. There was no Lazy Susan on this table.

Our breakfast the next day was rice noodles. Every time I managed to lift the noodles to cool, they slid off my chopsticks. After three or four attempts, and some laughter, I was given a spoon. Noodles are wet and my hand dexterity and strength were not there yet. I would suggest picking up two items as practice: wet noodles and roasted peanuts (no shells). If you pick up two peanuts at once, you will be praised for your marvelous chopstick skills because even locals have trouble doing that.

Later on that first week, we went to a countryside restaurant and ate alligator. This was my first experience with a round table and a Lazy Susan covering 75% of it. Fifteen co-workers attended so roughly 20 dishes were ordered. A safe rule of thumb is for every person at dinner to order one dish and at least one soup. Another new experience was everyone had their bowl, plate, teacup and alcohol cup shrink wrapped to show that it was from an official sterilizing company. Also, 300ml local fruit juice boxes were on the table, which surprised me.

The official first standing toast occurred and toasting continued throughout dinner. I observed co-workers toasting with laughter or a serious tone, depending on who was toasting who. Sometimes the toasts were with those seated next to each other, other times they were across the table even while everyone was talking. Sometimes people would stand, while others were told to sit and I couldn't figure out why they were trying so hard to keep the cups so low. It was all a bit overwhelming.

Eventually, I felt like it was my turn to toast others so I leaned over to my translator and asked what I was supposed to say. At first, she let me ramble on like I would at Thanksgiving dinner but after I said nearly the same thing to two different people, she rightfully cut me off and only afterward told me what "I said" to each person. As time went on and more dinner experience was gained, I figured out what they wanted to hear and kept things short, sweet, and flattering.

Fast forward a couple of years, and I'm still being invited to the hospital owner's big meetings. I think one of the strangest trends was being summoned to eat 10 minutes before the work shift ended with no prior notice or even 10 minutes into my meal prep at home. You can't really say you have plans; you get the call and you must go eat. We were trying to build a relationship with important people in the city, like top doctors or vice presidents from other hospitals in the bigger cities and so on. We had a mutual and somewhat unspoken agreement: he would look good having a foreigner at dinner and I did what you will learn in this book to make him and the hospital look really good.

This helped me become a big deal in the hospital. For a Chinese person to be able to hire an American, "a Western Foreigner", makes the owner gain a lot of face, especially in a smaller town like this. It reinforces what they can do and offer to entice a foreigner to leave their home country and work with them. That's unbelievable to some of the guests and I was an advertisement as well. I became known as "the guy who helps people with back and neck pain."

I wasn't this hospital's first Western hire so let me compare myself to the previous doctor who was very rigid, unwilling to adapt to the culture, always insisted on using a fork, only wanted to eat meat, and was a loud drunk. That doctor was only invited to eat when it was a departmental event or on other random occasions. I, on the other hand, was invited more regularly because I knew how to flatter the boss, the guests, and make everybody gain face.

We will learn all that is necessary to master the business dinner (and even make family or tourism dinners go smoothly) in the rest of the book. This was the moment I realized I knew what I was doing and should share all these tips: One day, I was invited to be a guest speaker at a Shanghai hospital, and we shared two meals in the hotel restaurant with seating for 25 at one table. The table and glass of the Lazy Susan were so big and heavy that it had a motor to keep it spinning at a steady pace. We are all sitting around enjoying our food and company and making toasts. I wasn't the only foreigner but I was honestly getting more smiles and toasts. The head of that hospital asked me for my WeChat code and offered me a monthly recurring consulting weekend job a week later. Making extra money for not a lot of effort is great and all because I understood the Chinese business dinner culture.

Fast forward a few months, and a friend was doing some of his own consulting in Shanghai. Me and my co-workers picked him up to share dinner and I started to quiz him on a few things that you will read in this book (the hosts don't speak English). He recognized some of the pearls in the book, but there were many things he didn't understand until I explained them to him. You could see the light bulbs turning on with the nuances I mentioned. Needless to say, he implemented the advice at his next dinner, got more positive engagement from his group, and ended up with a fantastic recommendation for his portfolio.

CHAPTER TWO:

RESTAURANT LAYOUT

Let me make a few assumptions before we continue. You are a pro at what you do and expanding into China helps meet your business goals. Let's also assume you've already made your contacts with Chinese businesspeople and you are either on a flight now or going to be coming over shortly. Lastly, your normal "work hour" dealings have been going well in person and now it's time to socialize over a table full of food and drinks.

I know you're no stranger to dinner tables but we're going to review a few that you will see on your trip to China. First, the most formal type is round and has a Lazy Susan on top (motorized or not) that fits 20 to 30 guests. The more usual and smaller round table will still have a Lazy Susan but will fit 8 to 12 guests. The last type you will encounter is square tables that fit 4 to 8 guests, normally in small restaurants, noodle diners, and less formal places. Some restaurants have a mix of tables but there are usually square tables in the middle and round tables on the perimeter, plus private rooms with their own door or privacy curtain.

Next up are the chairs. Some places will have exactly what you would expect: four legs with a cushion and a back cushion. A themed place might have a special style to fit their atmosphere. In nicer restaurants, chairs are covered with stretched cloth (what you might see at an American wedding). With noodle restaurants or other low-end budget places, you might see benches with no backs or little wooden stools no more than 12 to 18 inches tall. It's a safe bet that you will eat at places with "normal" chairs.

The star rating of the restaurant determines the silverware they use. If you're at a low-key restaurant, you should expect your bowls, plates, and drinking cups to be packaged in shrink wrap to let you know they are clean and sterilized. Every place is different but a bowl and at least a teacup are customary, though many places will have a clear glass for alcohol included in the shrink wrapped package. Chopsticks come in plastic sealed wrapping and will either be wooden, where you snap them apart from the top, or plastic. If you get the disposable wooden kind, after you separate them, you can rub the bottom four inches together to try and remove any rough edges. Splinters won't make for a fun dinner. Also, you will look like a local if you do this. If you have the hard plastic variety, just take them out of the wrapper and you are good to go.

More upscale places will have the chopsticks resting on the table next to your plate and bowl and nothing will be shrink-wrapped. You might have two plates with the bigger remaining in place and the smaller one on top will be used to discard your food scraps. This plate might be replaced halfway through the meal. At least one bowl will be in front of you. The chopsticks will usually be on your right and the tips will be resting on a small piece of porcelain or wood that match the plates and décor and are not touching the tablecloth directly. They may have a wine glass, a baijiu carafe with a cup to drink the baijiu, and a teacup. Baijiu is translated as white wine (Chardonnay has a different translation) and is made from rice. It's clear like vodka but can taste like rubbing alcohol.

Chopstick Protocol:

Since I'm describing the table and silverware right now, I find it only fitting to give you the top things you shouldn't do with your chopsticks if you want to keep face and get some contracts signed before you head back to your home country.

1. Don't stab your food with chopsticks. I know grabbing a potato or a dumpling can be tricky, but piercing food will make you look bad if someone notices. Always assume someone is watching you, or at least taking a peak.

2. Don't cross chopsticks over each other. Keep them parallel. You can place them across the top of your bowl or plate, but ensure they are next to each other and not crossing.

3. Don't point at anything with your chopsticks because you will look foolish and childlike. Point discretely with your finger.

4. You are staring at a bowl of mystery chicken and all you see is bone and skin. Deep down you want to push some out of the way and search for a piece of meat, but don't use your chopsticks to push food around. Remember, the chopsticks have been in your mouth so you should only grab the piece you want to eat and leave the rest untouched by your germs. Be patient and maybe the person next to you will clear the path. They love chewing on skin and bones.

5. Never lick the ends of your chopsticks. If you need to clean them, you can rub the tips in your rice. Another option is to slide the tip over the edge of your bowl to clean off whatever you don't want. The obvious choice is to wipe them with a napkin if you have a fresh one.

6. Chopsticks are not drumsticks so don't bang them on your dishes.

Bonus tip: Don't play on your phone during a meal. You may see others check their phones, but do your best not to. Boredom might set in if your translator isn't helping you understand the conversation going on around you, but still pay attention. Look interested, ask the translator questions, and leave the phone alone. I know it can get boring when everyone is speaking Chinese (Mandarin or pu tong hua). If you need to, excuse yourself to the bathroom and check your messages. This will be a 90 to 180 minute dinner after all.

When walking through the front of the restaurant, you may notice water tanks with fish, crabs, lobster and shellfish. A patron can pick a breed to be cooked for dinner while everyone else is making their way to the table. Now before you rush to sit down, read the next chapter so you can capitalize on the amazing business rapport you have already built.

CHAPTER THREE:

WHERE TO SIT AND BEGINNING OF DINNER

You are now in the restaurant (probably in a private room) and everyone is standing around. You will see the Lazy Susan table and there may already be food on it if someone pre-ordered it. Don't sit yet. Let me walk you through the seating arrangements.

If you're standing in the doorway looking directly across the table, that chair is for the number one person in the room so they are facing the door and can see everything that's going on. Left and right of that chair are the number two most important people and then two chairs away are number three. If you have your back against the door, you're the lowest rank in the group (even if you are the top person in your particular company). That's not to say you don't have power or you're not important, just that other people may outrank you or are choosing to honor other people in your group. If you are already established with the company and you're trying to court other businesses, you may find that you or your teammates aren't in the number one position. They'll probably put the person that you're trying to court in that position for honor and respect. Who gets the seat of honor will vary depending on your goals. It's quite possible that whoever you're trying to do business with will put you in this first or second position out of respect. You're the foreigner, you've come here, and they want to honor and respect you.

Someone might urge you towards a certain chair and say sit-sit though no one else is sitting yet. Just stand in front of it and indicate you understand but continue standing and chatting with others.

In Chinese culture, there tends to be a lot of offering and saying no before saying yes. Here are a few examples. Let's say you are at a convenience store with another Chinese person and you want a soda. You go to pay for it and they step in and try to pay. While they may ultimately pay for your soda, you have to say that you want to pay first. There will be some back and forth as they try to give the employee money, but concede and let them pay after the third time. If they are offering you a gift, be humble and say, "Oh no, not a gift. You shouldn't have." In this scenario, place your hand on the gift while it's in their hands and do a little push and shove / back and forth before you accept and thank them. The same applies when you give a gift. It's a fairly quick back and forth exchange but if you just accept the gift on the first offer, it indicates you're too eager.

Side note: When looking around a store or someone's house or office, be careful what you point at or ask questions about. When you inquire about an object, they assume you want it and might give it to you. At this point you will feel frustrated because you weren't asking for their possessions, just more information. Trust me from experience: be more indirect and casual when asking your translator about certain objects. For example, a friend was visiting a college for official business and pointed out some calligraphy that was around seven feet long hanging on the wall. Before they left, that calligraphy was removed from the frame, rolled up and put in a container for him as a gift. This calligraphy could easily have cost $7,000. My friend works at an American University so now it hangs in their halls. He didn't want the painting; he just took notice of it and wondered what it said. That's the generosity of the Chinese people.

The table itself will be round with a smaller diameter round glass on top (Lazy Susan). You might have a motorized tabletop that will spin around automatically but more than likely someone will manually turn it. When you are all seated, there should be multiple dishes around the edge of the glass. As time goes on, the wait staff will bring more dishes and fill up the entire table including the middle, unless it's a table for 20 or more people, as the center will have a floral arrangement.

The amount of dishes ordered typically depends on how many people are there. A ratio of 1 to 1 is pretty standard plus a soup or two. They will always order some hot dishes that are a mix of meat and vegetables as well as a few cold dishes of the same mix.

*Remember, you don't need to spin the Lazy Susan yourself. Be patient and wait for someone else to do it. A lower-ranking person may turn the table but that's not a hard rule because even the top person may decide to get to their favorite dish that's just out of reach. You shouldn't do that though. Also, never reach into someone else's personal space to get food. If it's too far away from you, wait for someone to turn the glass.

Once dinner has been going on for a little while, people will notice what you like to eat and might stop the table so you can get some more. They assume you will like certain dishes and will insist you try others so they can see your reaction. I'll discuss later how to grab your food, how to drink and toast, toasting orders and other details.

Sometimes all the food will have arrived, but no one is eating because they are waiting for somebody who is late. I've sat for 30 minutes waiting for one of the higher ranks to show up. It's frustrating when you're hungry, but there's not much you can do about it.

The plates will already be laid out in front of each chair between the edge of the table and the start of the Lazy Susan. If you have the shrink-wrapped variety instead, here's what to do. Don't be the first person to open it. Wait until others open theirs. Some people will use their chopsticks to quickly stab the plastic over the bowl and it will make a popping sound. If many people are doing it, have fun and do it as well. However, the alternative method is to just poke a hole with your finger (no pop) and pull the bowls and cups out.

What do you do with the plastic? See what the other

guests are doing. I'm confident they will just throw it on the floor underneath their chair at their feet and push it under the table a little. You don't want to slip on it when you stand and toast throughout dinner, so that's why you push it out of your feet's way.

At this point, I assume everyone is seated and someone is pouring tea and then the inevitable alcohol situation occurs. You can assume beer will not be served and it will be red wine if you're lucky. Unfortunately, if you are a male, you will probably have to forego the red wine and drink a 'manly' baijiu, which is 40-55% proof clear rice wine alcohol (like vodka and gin) but translates to English as white wine. Don't assume you're getting a glass of Chardonnay when someone asks if you want Chinese white wine. The baijiu glass will be filled to the brim. Each glass is 2.5 shots and three or four will mean a rough night and tough following day. In a culture where drinking glass for glass can show respect and some people don't mind saying they need help walking, it's best to take it slow. In the following chapter, I will talk more about drinking and how to fake it a little too.

Now everyone has their two drinks (tea and alcohol), but wait until the head person makes the introductory toast before you eat or drink. The number one person will stand up, then everyone else stands up and a short speech or toast will be made. When they are done, they will motion everyone to sit down and eat. Once you notice people putting their chopsticks into their food, you are free to eat. Don't drink alcohol unless you are asked to toast or you are toasting someone else. Again, the next chapter will explain this all in detail. When the meal and socializing are coming to end, be sure to keep a little baijiu in your cup because you will need to drink the rest of it for the final toast that ends dinner.

CHAPTER FOUR:

TOASTING, DRINKING, AND SMOKING

Unlike most western countries, it's very rude to sip your alcohol without first toasting someone. I know the food in China is typically spicy and you want to cool your mouth down, so make sure you have water, juice, tea, soda, whatever, as your normal drink. I wouldn't use the baijiu to cool my mouth down and you usually won't have a cold beer (in fact they may serve them room temperature) so enjoy that warm tea and water.

We'll go over the toasting order in a minute, but first an important question. Should you sit or stand while giving and/or receiving a toast? Well, as a general rule, the first and last toast by the head of the group will be made standing and so will you. The rest of the toasts, as I will discuss, depend on the person you're toasting. Just push your chair back a little to give yourself space to stand up in front of the chair. As you will probably be making many toasts, you may choose to sit more on the edge of your seat, so you don't have to push your chair in and out all night.

21

Showing respect to another person allows them and yourself to keep and gain face. When someone is prompting you to toast with them, make the gesture and start to stand up. Depending on that person, they will either stand up as well or motion you to sit down. If you are motioned to sit down, then go ahead and sit but you will still have to 'hold the cup', which I will explain soon. You want to test standing with each person; some people's egos are bigger than others and they want that respect. If someone's going to toast you and they are already standing, you need to stand too.

Toast Order

The toast order will vary based on where you sit and who you're eating with. After the boss gives the initial toast, you all start eating. Start looking around and you'll notice that the person in the second rank seats will toast the number one seat within a few minutes. Then the number two seats will toast the third seats next to them. The number one seat will slowly toast his way around the table. At the same time, everyone at the table will find their time to toast with the number one seat. Then they will toast the second then third and so on. Your job in regards to where you're sitting is to make sure that you end up toasting everybody at the table starting with the highest-ranked.

Since everyone is eating and trying to toast in the same order, it can take 30 minutes to finish the first round. The boss is eating and talking and in-between bites and sips they are doing the rounds while also accepting toasts from all the guests. Be patient, because you will be doing the same thing.

> *Remember, you have to initiate toasts with everyone even though you already drank with them from their invitation.

Skipping someone is considered very disrespectful as they will think that you don't have enough respect for them and that could compromise any business deals you're trying to secure.

When there are 10-15 people at dinner and food and conversation continues for 90-180 minutes, you will notice who is getting more toasts than the rest. Once you finish toasting everyone, that's the person you want to make sure to drink with a few extras times. Don't neglect the smaller players, but you may toast some people twice and others three or four times. You don't want any gossip behind your back or in front of your face if you can't understand Mandarin.

Everyone is eating while all these toasts occur. You may not remember everyone's name to get their attention. If you have a translator present, discreetly ask who the person you want to toast is. Even the translator may not remember, but if you want the guy in the blue shirt, they will know how to get their attention politely. Chinese people use all kinds of names for unfamiliar people: uncle, aunt, sir, boss, president, etc. even if you aren't related.

Also, since everyone is eating, be aware that the person you want to toast may have just started chewing. Wait a second before interrupting. This scenario will happen to you more often than you would like. Therefore, as a courtesy, I recommend not doing it to others. It's a sad moment when you have a delicious bite and then have to drink baijiu with your mouth full.

*Be aware, if someone just put a bite of food in their mouth, wait a moment before you toast.

Another thing to be careful about is initiating a toast immediately after they toasted another person. Hold off a minute and then toast. You could skip position three and go to position four with only a slight risk of offending that person. However, there could be multiple people with the same rank and then it's just a matter of catching all of them and not leaving anyone out. If you're trying to keep everything straight in your head, just wait a minute, then toast. You don't want to initiate the second chair then the opposite end of the table and back again.

You want to sip the baijiu as often as you can, compared to taking ¼ of the cup with each toast. It's 50% alcohol. One glass is 2.5 shots and they always want to refill your glass. Some people will pressure you to drink more to test you. Someone might think it's funny or cool to get people drunk so keep an eye open for that person. Drinking too much is a sign of respect for some, but I think it's ridiculous. You probably want to pace yourself and consume only two glasses, unless you like getting drunk then have three, or wasted to the point of barely walking and throwing up then indulge in four or more. I'm not a fan of getting drunk; it's a business meeting, so two would probably be a good limit.

*Never tell them how many beers or baijiu you can drink. If you say one or two, some individuals will push you to your stated limit and add extra. Don't end up in a hospital getting your stomach pumped trying to show off. I will teach you some tricks to fake drink later on and I can coach you with a video how to use water to fine-tune those trickery skills.

How to Hold the Cup

You should grip under the lip/top of the cup with the right hand using the thumb and second and third fingers. The fourth and fifth fingers either hover under the cup or are placed slightly back compared to the other two fingers. Your left hand is palm up in a relaxed position underneath the cup as if it was a saucer and the cup will slightly hover over the fingers, not the center of the palm.

Regardless of whether you're standing or sitting for a toast, the next few motions are the same. Hold the cup and raise your arms somewhere between nipple level and the top of the collar bone. This area is your starting point. Face whoever is speaking with the cup held correctly and in the upper chest area. Listen to the person giving the toast and show your interest. That could mean a slight smile but no teeth showing or you may have a more enthusiastic face if the evening is getting lively.

Unless you speak Mandarin, you won't understand what is being said at the toasts. Hopefully, a translator will be nearby to whisper what they are saying. The translator probably won't do it in real-time or give you a word for word account, but will give you a synopsis when the person finishes. Regardless of whether you get a translation during or after, you will do two things when they stop.

1. Almost everyone will give a 3 inch downward shift of the head, a nod. However, it's not a deep bend with your entire upper body, as that's more of a Japanese thing. The Chinese way is more like an exaggerated up-down head nod.

2. What should you do with your arms? If you are standing you will bring your arms from the upper chest area, down to the bellybutton level or several inches above the table. Look around and you will see everybody is dropping their arms and hands first, and then raising back up to take a sip (keeping the hands around the cup as discussed earlier).

3. The big takeaway is to match the height of the person toasting you but go a little lower to honor that person.

If you are toasting around the table and sitting instead of standing, the principles are similar but with a few differences. You start with the cup high and then bring it lower before taking a sip. In the seated scenario, match however low the other person brings their cup to show more respect. You both may bring it level with the table, your bowl, the Lazy Susan, or touch the rim of a dish on the Lazy Susan. In some instances, hover just above the surfaces mentioned and other times lightly tap the surface. Some people try to integrate the western style of touching each other's cups but that's generally not the case.

The default should be to bring the cup to the level of a dish on the Lazy Susan and if they go lower try and match their level. Of course, there are always exceptions but again a good rule of thumb is to observe what others are doing and follow suit. Sometimes it feels like a game of who can go lower with the cup.

As the night goes on, you can imagine the atmosphere will become less formal. People have had too much to drink but you still have to toast correctly. The problem is drunken people have different personalities, so someone might get extra pushy for you to drink the entire cup at once, also known as ganbei or bottoms up.

"Ganbei" translates to bottoms-up, cheers, and finish what's in your cup in one gulp. Now obviously that's not something you want to be doing all night long, especially with every guest so you need to do the following. Just smile and say, "Oh, no, no, no" and try to play it off saying, "I'm not able to drink as much as you. Please let's just drink a little." Another phrase I like to say during these times is, "Yi dian dian" (pronounced like e-d-ian-d-ian), which means a little, so throw that in and put your thumb and second finger close together (like a pinch of salt) to illustrate the 'just a little' sign. I hope that you can now get away with much less.

Hopefully, there won't be anyone there who just wants to get you drunk. Some just want to see how much you can drink as that shows respect (regardless of whether you think it's stupid, it's their culture, not yours). Again, if you're in a big city, there is less of that mentality. To sum it up, my goal is always to take little sips, even if it looks like I took more. One of my tricks to make it look like I took a decent sip is to just make the 'that's a strong flavor face' but in reality, you didn't even drink.

That trick will help your cup last a lot longer.

At the end of the meal, the leader will toast and the cups will be expected to be emptied. Again, make sure you leave a little bit in your cup so you have something to drink later. If not, someone will come around and do a last call refill. If you have some left, you can wave your hand over your cup and that will tell them you are good. You can usually tell the dinner is coming to end because people have generally stopped eating and it has turned into a conversation around the table.

Last thought: When your cup is getting low, someone will want to refill it. Just let them refill it once or twice and keep track of how much you drank so you don't exceed two full cups. You could even say 'ban' which means half, so they only fill it half way. This gesture will go a long way into making them like you.

Dinner Buzz Words in Chinese

Here are some words that you probably want to learn:

That's delicious = hao chi (how ch-er , the ch- of chair and -er of receiver). You will be asked Hao Chi Ma – Is it delicious? – often so learn to say hao chi. You may also here hao chi bu hao chi, which means is it delicious or not.

Take a shot, bottoms up = ganbei. (gan has a soft 'A' sound, it would not be as strong as the 'A' in can. Bei is pronounced like bay).

Thank you = xiexie (pronounced like she she).

I'm full = chi bao le (the chi is the same as before. Bao sounds like bow and le is like the French le or the le in letter.)

Half way = ban (said like the bon in Bon Jovi).

Don't smoke = bu chou yan (bu is similar to the way 'you' is pronounced or boo as in the Halloween scary phrase. Chou has the 'O' sound like NO with the ch of chair. You could also say it like 'Row' but with the CH-OW). Yan sounds like can). Chinese is very much a smoking culture. If you smoke, great, go on and smoke with them. If you don't smoke, say Bu Chou Yan, Xiexie and wave your hand to show the NO emphasis.

Not smoking is not a big deal to them, but do expect multiple people to offer you a cigarette throughout dinner.

Look around and you will see people take a cigarette from someone else and probably use someone else's lighter. Extra respect points if they let the other person light it for them. Stay strong with your no and you won't have to smoke.

Your Toasting Phrases

When you're giving a toast, you don't have to be overly creative. You only need to say one sentence. I'm not even going to write these in Mandarin. Have your translator rework what you said and they can say it to the group.

Here is a list of common phrases to say: wish them good health; wish that their family will be healthy; you could mention you hope their kids pass their big exams; here's to our business relationship and that it will be profitable for both parties; this city is very nice; your office/factory is beautiful; your leadership skills are good; your staff members have made you feel very welcome; you are an excellent host and you feel very welcome; the food here is great but the company is better; here's to having a long-lasting business relationship; we are taking the right steps together; our partnership is going to be great for everyone involved. If they ask whether you like China or if you think the opposite gender of Chinese people are attractive, just say yes to both.

If you feel at a loss for what to say, ask your translator and they should be able to help. They go to formal dinners all the time and know the top ten most common phrases and should be able to pick an appropriate one based on the vibe of the meeting.

Fake Drinking

If you are reading this and saying, "I don't like drinking or I don't like getting drunk," awesome, me neither, so here are some pointers to try and fake drink on some of the toasts.

You can try and be sneaky once you are halfway through the first cup. Put the cup to your mouth, let a little hit your tongue and swallow as if you drank. After you drank a little, you will know how strong the taste is and make a point to remember the face you made or the outward reaction you made. Use a less intense version of that when you fake it. Warning, if you burp later that night, it will taste like baijiu.

If you notice you've already gotten close to your limit and are buzzing, you will need to slow your drinking down in a hurry. One option is to put a little in your mouth and fake swallow. Next bring, your half-full teacup to your mouth as if you need to wash the baijiu down, but instead of drinking, discreetly spit the baijiu into your teacup. This option is a bit riskier and grosser. You don't want to be obvious because that's going to be considered rude and you will lose face. This is more of a last-ditch effort if you're trying to be polite without actually saying, "NO, I'm done drinking." Remember, you might be a guest but you still have self-control and can say NO to drinking. You are not forced to do anything you don't want to do.

*The biggest thing you can do is consistently say yi dian dian and take small sips.

As the dinner progresses, someone will come around to refill your cup. Just try and wave them off or put your hand on top of the glass. You might get some resistance so you can play the no game and then let them fill it up the first time or just half way.

Smoking

If you're lucky, maybe you will be in a major city with people who don't smoke. However, in my experience, there is always at least one person who does. Rarely will you find a restaurant that has a strict no smoking policy, especially if you are in a private room.

Assume people will smoke and your clothes will smell like cigarettes after dinner. If you're allergic to the smoke or just react poorly to second-hand smoke or pollution causes you trouble, then I would advise you to figure out what relieves your symptoms before you come here. If medicines help, then don't forget them at home.

People will offer each other cigarettes and many will take them. Usually, one person will walk around the table and offer everyone a cigarette. If you take it, they will probably try and light it for you. It's respectful for you to let them light it. You might want to cup your hand around it to block any wind and after it is lit, use your pinky finger to tap their hand to indicate it's lit and to thank them. After that first round of cigarette offering, normally if one person near you wants to smoke, they will offer other people one first and light theirs last.

If you do smoke and you brought your cigarettes, be sure to offer them. They will love to try your western brand but don't be surprised if they think the Chinese made are better and tell you why.

As mentioned in the common phrases to learn section, if you don't smoke, say bu chou yan, xie xie (I don't smoke, thank you). Also, you can put your hand up and give the NO wave along with the no head motion. No need to exaggerate these motions; just doing them along with those Chinese words will be enough for them to move on. Alternatively, instead of the wave, you can put both hands together as if you're praying and rotate your hands back and forth with your arms in a fixed position and say bu chou yan, xie xie. This would be the most respectful way to decline a cigarette.

I don't think it will come to this situation but let's pretend that you are being pressured to smoke. What should you do? Take the cigarette and light it. After that, you can just hold it and let it burn while keeping it out of eyesight at table level or just below it. Perhaps bring it to your mouth two or three times to pretend to smoke but not inhale. After a few minutes and when people are distracted, you can just drop it at your feet, which is why I said to hold it out of eyesight.

Let's say you just had a cigarette and you're offered another. You can do the Yes- No game, take it, and put it behind your ear or rest it on the table. Look around and see what other people do so you can follow suit. They understand if you just finished smoking and need a break.

I'm not going to start smoking because it's a horrible habit and I don't want to get cancer or emphysema later in my life. So I just deny it and move on. For what it's worth, airports, hospitals, and subways have signs encouraging people to quit smoking and that it's bad for your heart and lungs.

Now, let's go to the next chapter, where we talk about eating food, chopsticks, and more.

CHAPTER FIVE:

EATING ETIQUETTE

Let's talk about the food, how to eat, and the proper etiquette when it comes to the food part of dinner, not just the drinking. If you need any more help, want to see it in action, or have personal questions, reach out at drtrosclair@gmail.com or JustinTrosclairMCC on Facebook©. I find it fun and I love to help so contact me.

If you don't already know how to use chopsticks (kuai zi), I would highly suggest you visit your nearest sushi and Chinese restaurants and start practicing.

Have you noticed at Chinese restaurants that the food is always bite-size? You aren't going to find a 16 oz. ribeye steak at 99% of the restaurants in China. That's because they don't use forks and knives regularly. In fact, in my entire five years of living in China, I never owned a single fork. Therefore, all your meat and vegetables are cut into the thin strips that can be easily lifted with chopsticks. These small pieces also help your food cook so much faster. Next time you cook at home, chop eggplant into cubes, Julienne some potatoes and carrots, slice some beef and stir fry it yourself. You'll be amazed at how fast it cooks and then take out your chopsticks and practice before flying over. Trust me, they will be impressed if you can use them instead of asking for a fork.

Rest assured that the places you will eat will have a ceramic soup type spoons. Soup is always served, so they provide you with a proper utensil. If you start using that spoon to eat other food, you might get laughed at. Some dishes will have a serving spoon and it's acceptable to use that to spoon it into your bowl.

I have one exercise for you to try at home. Get a bag of unshelled peanuts and pour them onto a plate. Build your finger dexterity by lifting a peanut with chopsticks and placing them in your mouth or another bowl closer to you. If you want to gain even more respect for your skills, learn how to lift two peanuts at the same time. As I mentioned, even locals have a hard time doing that. Hint: The trick is constant pressure.

By the time you get to China, you will be a master and they will definitely make comments on your skills and ask how you got so good.

How to Hold Chopsticks

Watch a 'how-to' video on YouTube® to get a visual step by step best practice on holding chopsticks. I have a video on this as well; just type my name and chopsticks. People have different finger positions, so I'll share the common concepts below.

The bottom chopstick is your stabilization utensil. It should rest on the pad (fingerprint area) and the top tip of your ring finger (fourth finger). The other side is on the web between your first (thumb) and second finger. That is the base chopstick and it doesn't move, the top chopstick is the one that does the 'pinching'.

The top chopstick is held with your thumb pad and the first and second fingertips gripping it while also having part of the chopstick resting on top of the web (or bottom of second finger) next to the bottom chopstick.

I keep the top chopstick resting on the web and the fingerprint area of my thumb. Then I keep my first and second fingers touching each other and use my thumb to push the chopstick against the middle of the two fingerprint area.

The big trick is pressure. The thumb and two fingers are pressing/squeezing the top chopstick while the fourth finger (supporting the bottom chopstick) is squeezing in and slightly up. It's this two-directional counter force that keeps a good grip on the food so you can successfully raise it into your mouth. This is why I recommended practicing at home, particularly with the peanuts to gain dexterity and strength.

Once you have the chopsticks in position, you may notice that the tips (the side you would pick up food with) don't line up. That would make gripping food difficult so loosen your grip, and have both tips touch your plate to line them up. Now that the ends meet, redo your grip.

Noodles are tough. You have 18 inches of noodles and you finally see the end, but they are slippery. Don't ask for a fork though. Someone will see you struggling and help you out. Just let them. Actually, in many cases, someone will anticipate that you will struggle. It takes a while to get used to picking up noodles. They are heavy, slippery, and long.

How Should I Serve Myself

The first toast is finished, you're sitting down, and you can't wait to eat. The next step is whether the leader will take a bite of food or motion for everyone to eat. Most people know the word eat, so you might hear people around you say 'Eat-Eat'. Sometimes you are urged so fast you didn't even have time to pick up and properly grip the chopsticks. Don't panic or be embarrassed; just adjust and enjoy the food. This section will explain how to serve yourself.

Think about Christmas dinner for a minute. Your family has 15 dishes and a spoon in each dish. Everyone goes around with their plate and puts however much of each on their plate. China, however, is a bit different. Those same 15 dishes will be on the Lazy Susan and your plates will be empty, but that's where the similarity ends.

All 15 guests will use their chopsticks to take the food they want from each dish, but only in the amount that can fit into their mouth as one bite. Then when each person wants another bite, they use those same chopsticks and grab a little more from the dish in front of them. If you think this sounds a lot like double-dipping, you are correct but it's more like 20 dippings. It may sound gross and perhaps it is, but the thing you have to remember is that you're trying to only touch what you are about to eat. If you use your chopsticks to push the fatty meat out of your way to get the meat only piece, that's considered rude and gross because you touched so many other pieces.

Let me give you a better viewpoint. A plate of green beans cut into chopstick manageable pieces are right in front of you as well as an eggplant dish to your left and a pork dish on your right. All three dishes are available for you to eat without having to invade your neighbor's personal space. You decide to pick up a green bean first. You grab it with your amazing skills and directly eat it. If the piece is big, you grabbed too much or it's slippery and you are about to drop it, then go ahead and put it in your bowl then eat it. Now you want to try the pork dish. Don't clean the ends of the chopsticks or dip them in water. Just go on and pick a piece of pork up and put in in your mouth. Everyone else will be doing the same thing.

One piece of etiquette to remember is to not lick or suck the food end (or any piece really) of the chopsticks. If you find your tips are messy, you can swipe them in your bowl of rice. The rice will pick up the mess but please do this discreetly. Picking up a piece of rice to eat can sometimes accomplish the same thing. Of course you can use a napkin and clean off the ends if you so desire.

Another tip: Most westerns don't want a big piece of fatty meat; we want muscle. Check the dish and find the piece you want without pushing all the pieces around. As mentioned earlier, that is rude, childish behavior. It's like contaminating the rest of the food.

An important fact to remember: Tabletops aren't considered very clean or sterile. Maybe where you are from, if you dropped a French fry on the table you would pick it up and still eat it. In China, if you drop something on the table, any part of the table, do not pick it up again. Just let it go. Even if it was the best piece you could find; just mourn the loss for a second and move on. Don't try to pick it back up, just get another piece. This is sage advice 9 out of 10 times.

*If you drop food on the table, do not pick it back up to eat.

How Much Food to Take

Again, only take what you can fit in your mouth. Don't stockpile enough potato for the evening or fill your bowl full of stir-fried beef and peppers. Luckily, some dishes will have a spoon. For instance, ground beef with chopped peppers is difficult for anyone to pick up with chopsticks. In this case, a spoon will be on the dish and you can grab one or two spoonfuls and put it in your bowl. Have some rice with that beef and peppers and mix it all up.

*Assume any spoon in a dish is a serving spoon.

At least one type of soup will be served with a meal with a ladle. Typically someone will take the responsibility and try to serve everyone a bowl of the chicken or beef soup. They will ask for your bowl and serve you. Expect the chicken soup to contain the feet and head. Kindly wave off the head if you don't want to eat and it's offered. Beef will have some organ meat so keep an eye out for what's in your bowl. They love the broth and it's honestly delicious. Green leafy vegetables (lettuce, spinach, etc.) will come boiled in a bowl. Use your chopsticks to grab a piece.

A meat dish that looks like lots of meat and not fat is usually what a Westerner is hoping for. That meat might be fried or in a soup. Once that dish is in front of you, assess how much others have been eating. If it seems to be popular and it looks like the best dish to you, go ahead and grab a few extra pieces. Sometimes a dish won't make it back around, but that's usually dumplings or bread. Another exception is leafy vegetables. You could purposely or accidentally grab too much, so just put it in your bowl and enjoy those few extra bites.

Where to Put the Bones and Other Waste

Your plate is the discard area (or the table itself in some restaurants). The bones from the ribs, fish, etc. are placed on the plate if it's available. The wait staff will at some point replace it with a new one when it's getting full. You eat out of the bowl, so try not to discard things in it.

If you are in a less fancy place, put your scraps on the table itself. Some places are so low key that you can drop it on the floor. As I say many times in this book, observe what others are doing and follow. Throwing the plastic wrapping from your bowl and cup under the table is quite common. It feels odd to us, but when you see everyone else doing, you know you can too. Look around and see if people are putting the waste on the table or the plate. The small noodle restaurants are where you might expect to throw napkins and waste on the floor. It's a strange thing but you adapt quickly.

A common thing while you wait to eat the meal is to have plain sunflower seeds. If you're at a table and there are sunflower seeds and you want to eat some, you normally put the shells on the floor. They eat sunflower seeds one at a time, by breaking it with their front teeth, releasing the seed, and then throwing it away. It's not like the American way when we put a handful of seeds in our mouth and just spit them as you go. Sunflower seeds and peanuts are pretty common to see at a meal and the shells are tossed on the floor. Someone will sweep up all the trash at the end of the meal.

Food Topics

Meat: When you get to China, you will notice that beef will have plenty of fat and chicken and fish are served with the bones. It may be unfamiliar to put that piece of chicken and bone in your mouth and suck it clean. Usually, we hold it with our hand or partially hold it with a chopstick and our hand and then eat around the bone.

Whatever method you choose will be just fine. Once finished, discard the bone.

*Chicken and duck are chopped into roughly one-inch pieces so you won't be able to tell if it's the thigh, neck, or breast, but expect bones to be present in each bite.

Fish have little bones hiding in the meat. So after you gracefully pull the skin back with a chopstick in your bowl, bite slowly and chew softly to avoid getting a bone stuck in your throat. This could be a bad situation if it punctures your intestines so remember to chew slowly. If you already see bones sticking out, pull them out, preferably with chopsticks, or your fingers.

One of the special parts to be offered is the chicken or fish head. Some people enjoy gnawing on those areas. If you know you have no intention of even touching those parts, waive it off convincingly. I would even tell the translator, "Oh no, I really won't eat it. I appreciate the gesture but please give it to someone who will eat it." That will usually be enough for them to skip you.

Also, chicken and duck feet are delicious items for locals. I don't care to eat the skin and ligaments but go for it if you want to. There are plenty of bones you will need to spit out on your plate. Since eating chicken feet is pretty messy, couples on dates usually avoid them.

The fun of Chinese culinary feasts would not be complete without some dishes you don't even want to try. For instance, a dish of fried fat (just think of a half inch thick piece of fat and it's not crackling), a pork dish with fresh blood, cooked blood served in cubes, or even fried bees and worms. Different cultures have different foods. Some people will eat it, some will take a single bite, and some won't touch it. Here comes the bad news. If it seems wild and it's served on a dish, someone will probably pressure you to try it. If you can, find the least gross part, and eat it quickly. Hopefully, you can get away with a smaller piece, play along, and look good in the process.

Once the rhythm of the meal is underway and the food is spinning around, you may notice that your favorite dishes are enjoyed by others as well. Next time it passes in front of you, grab a piece or two extra because it may not make it back around. If you see that there is a limited supply of a dish, like dumplings or pot stickers, do the math so you can see if you can eat two, but check because they may order just enough for everyone. Don't be greedy and lose face. Lastly, if you're trying something new, you might take a small bite first. That way if you end up not liking it, you're not wasting something others would love to eat.

Fruit is generally served at the beginning as a snack, especially if you go to someone's house or maybe an office. Some restaurants will bring it after the meal, so it's more like a dessert. I can't recall ever getting a 'dessert' menu. There will be no chocolate cake, cobblers, bread pudding, after-dinner coffee, etc. offered at the meal. If you're lucky, there might be some fried golden bread to dip into evaporated sweetened milk.

Rice is usually brought in midway through the meal. My general rule of thumb with rice is, if there is a dish that makes sense to mix with the rice (think jambalaya or 'rice dressing'. Yes, I'm from South Louisiana) then I will serve myself a half bowl of rice during the meal. Other than that, there are so many main dishes you could overeat. You may feel odd not getting rice when everyone is on their second bowl, but again, I want to eat these special dishes that you can only find in China. Of course, if you're drinking more baijiu than you're comfortable with, a bowl of rice could help slow the absorption.

Eating rice is quite easy because it sticks together. However, when you get down to the bottom of the bowl and it's mixed with the different sauces the rice becomes wet and not very chopstick friendly. The remedy is to bring the bowl to your mouth and use the chopsticks to shovel it in. It will look like you are drinking the milk after you ate your breakfast cereal. Other guests might make some slurping noises but don't feel obligated to reciprocate. Drinking soup is pretty much the same. The first few spoonfuls will have vegetables or meat and then you can just drink the soup from the bowl.

Dietary Restrictions

You are a foreigner and they expect you to be a meat-eater. If you are a vegetarian, just know that everything will pretty much be cooked either with a little pork for flavor or a mixture of cooking oil and a little animal fat.

If you're a vegan, I would just suggest putting your beliefs on the shelf for a week and eat as vegetarian as you can. It's only for a short amount of time to close a business deal. Generally thinking, they will not understand why you wouldn't eat animals. They can understand being vegetarian because for some it's a religious thing and others have a digestive issue. If you are picky, you will be considered annoying and it will hurt the business relationship.

Allergies are a whole other ball game. If you are allergic to shellfish then please tell someone. They might take you to a seafood restaurant if they don't know. If there is some ingredient that you can't eat or be around, again, mention it before they order. Nobody wants to see you stab yourself with an epi-pen halfway through dinner.

I had a vegetarian friend accompany me to a relaxed business dinner. About half the dishes he didn't eat because it was a pure meat dish, but he still tried a couple of vegetable dishes (cooked with pork) after they put a little pressure on him. He took just a few bites and the other guests were happy. One dish was an orange crab soup served in an orange. He just ate it even though if he eats too much meat it may cause a stomach ache. After dinner, I told him how much I appreciated him not making a big fuss about it all and nobody lost face.

To Sum It Up

Every dish will not be what you want to eat. Don't just put your chopsticks down and cross your arms and look bored or not toast. Just find something that you can pick at and stay engaged. Even if you don't know what is being said, pay attention to the body language of everyone and get your translator to give you a recap of what's going on. Don't forget that during all this eating you will also be toasting. They will order more food that can be eaten so don't worry about the waste. Pace yourself with the alcohol because dinners can last 90 minutes or more.

Remember, when you're going through the toasting, put your chopsticks down. Don't point with chopsticks; just rest them on top of your bowl. Be courteous to everyone, show them respect, try the food, sip the wine, smile, enjoy yourself, and close the deal.

BONUS CHAPTER

The Tea Ceremony

No Chinese experience is complete without having a tea ceremony on a decorative plank of wood. Below is the general layout of what you will see and what to expect. This is a much more simple procedure than you might imagine and when sipping tea with business people, you don't have to worry about buying any afterward. Smoking will be involved with men present and the same rules apply as dinner.

Unlike dinner, there is no official seating arrangement. They will point to a chair for you to sit in. The person brewing and pouring the tea will sit across the table from everyone else.

Chinese businesspeople have some elaborate tea tables that will usually be about mid-thigh in height. They might be a big slab of wood with some intricate carvings on the top and sides. It could be the trunk of a tree with the top carved out flat. They have other varieties like simple trays on a table, but businesspeople will have a wooden glossy tea table with a flat top.

The top of the wood will be cut flat and the center will be carved deeper so you have a rim. The top will also be slightly sloped and you will see a drain. Also on the top of the table will be a special hot plate that will have a water spigot to pour water into a kettle and then boil it. Teacups, tea kettle, tea leaf holder and drainer, the tweezers and tea poker and the tea toys will be in that carved out area. The drain is there for a reason I will explain shortly.

Some people decorate their tea table with little statues. They could be dragons, pig figurines, and so on. One particular item is the turtle. The turtle will be facing away from the door, meaning money won't go out the door. This is the most popular tea toy.

How to Brew Tea

While the water is boiling, they will put the appropriate amount of tea leaves into a tea kettle. Once the water is boiled, the host will pour it over all the teacups as a way to wash it. Sometimes they will fill one cup, grab it with tea tweezers, swirl it around and then pour it into the next cup. They may fill one cup and then put each cup in that water, especially the rim to clean them all. Once the host is satisfied, he will boil more water.

Once the water is ready, the host will fill up the tea kettle that has the tea and put the lid on it then almost immediately pour the tea out on the table and the drain will whisk it away. This is washing the leaves. The next step is to fill the tea kettle up again. Now they will have a second tea kettle with some kind of filter resting on top.

They pour the tea through the filter (so it catches the sediment and potentially any leaves) into the second kettle. Finally, the tea is ready to be poured into everyone's small teacups. All of these products come in different shapes, sizes, materials, and colors.

Those pots are hot so kudos to them for being able to grab them barehanded. Your fresh tea is boiling water. Wait a few seconds before you sip it and blow on it first. The cup itself might be hot so just be careful. The cup is small so you only need to cradle it with the thumb and first two fingers.

How to Sip Tea

Now the cup is in your hand, bring it to your mouth and nose area and smell it a little. Much like smelling a glass of wine, see if you can recognize anything. Then take a small sip. Let it sit on your tongue for a few seconds to get a sense of the flavor and then swallow. You could have a different flavor when the tea touches your lips, tongue, back of the throat, and finally the after taste. This isn't iced tea that you gulp down on a hot summer day. It's a hot beverage that should be enjoyed slowly.

You'll see that they drink it slowly. Most teacup sizes only hold two or three sips. Once you put it down, they fill it back up. The boiling of water, pouring over the leaves and then straining will be repeated until the tea is almost just water flavor. People talk during the tea ceremony and fruit and seeds may be offered. This is not a complicated situation as a guest. Just talk, sip tea, and enjoy a tradition that goes back thousands of years.

Thank you again, for reading and hope you enjoyed this bonus chapter. I wish you much success for your next business dinner and tea with Chinese colleagues. Go close that deal and write a review on Amazon about how the book helped you.

I want to thank you so much for reading this book. This is what you need to know without unnecessary stories and in-depth cultural lessons. I hope that after reading this book you can reflect on past trips and see what you did well or not. Also, for those headed to China for the first time, I hope you see all the things I talked about and that dinner culture just flows out of you like a local. The pictures are a helpful reminder in mastering business dinners for Chinese businesspeople. Business dinners help determine if you're friendly and trustworthy, so the things that you can do to avoid your embarrassment, save your face, save their face, and potentially impress them with these nuances will go a long way. They will be impressed with you because you did your homework. You did your due diligence.

If you are going alone or in a group and you want to do a video chat for how some of these principles play themselves out, contact me. If you need me to fly out to your place of business for personal or group training, I can do that as well. It won't be the first time that someone's called, and I love these chats. So please don't hesitate in making the best impression you can and getting more business. My email again is drtrosclair@gmail.com. Let's get something scheduled.

OTHER BOOKS BY
DR. JUSTIN TROSCLAIR, D.C.

I've written several other books during my time in China.

Today's Choices, Tomorrow's Health

The first is called Today's Choices, Tomorrow's Health: small steps to improve your health, food choices, exercise, and life. It can be found at www.adoctorsperspective.net/tcth or on Amazon®. It was a number one bestseller for a little while and peaked at 105 on all of Kindle®.

As a chiropractic doctor (a seven to eight year program), part of the book will discuss what that profession can do for your health: what pain is, why we have pain, can it ever be a good thing, and how to get rid of it. As an evidence-based chiropractor, you won't see anti-vaccine rhetoric and the services I provide are known to get results. Contrary to popular belief, I don't want to see you forever, now back to the book.

I discuss my own 25-pound weight loss journey and ways I have found to keep it off. I went from not exercising and weightlifting to being able to perform cardio for 30 minutes, weightlifting exercise routines, and now enjoy going to the gym. Does hating exercise sound familiar to you? For many that is their story.

As many people say, weight loss is based on the diet (eating food), not the gym. It doesn't matter if you run 90 minutes a day if you're eating four donuts for breakfast. I found different ways to help trick myself into feeling full and not eating as much. Some tips are from research, client experiences, and lessons from China.

You can learn about some of the top ways to do intermittent fasting. It has huge benefits so you can experiment with some of the regimens mentioned. Another question I hear a lot is, "How much should I eat?" Instead of blindly recommending 1600 calories, I found several formulas that will give you exactly how many calories you should eat per day and can even factor in exercise. Now every week you can redo your daily calorie max.

Another hot topic is ketogenic diets and eating the optimal percentage of macros (protein, fat, and carbs). Again, I present information to help guide you through these topics.

Lastly, I give you 12 different exercises and stretches, blueprints to reduce headaches and strengthen your back so you can help keep back pain away and sleep better.

Finally, one of my passions is budgeting and finances and since most Americans hold a lot of debt and money is a huge cause for divorce, I wrote a lengthy section on it.

We'll go through many types of expenses, how to get on a budget, and even retirement options. Pick up this book on Amazon right now.

Needle-less Acupuncture

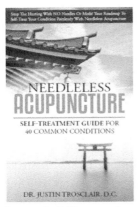

The second book is a do it yourself no-needle acupuncture (www.adoctorsperspective.net/bundlepacks) for 40 common conditions. You could call this acupressure if you were so inclined. In China, I worked as a chiropractor in the Traditional Chinese Medicine department and nearly every patient received acupuncture. You also see lots of different charts for conditions in China as well as manuals from the USA. So I went through and combined East meets West acupuncture theory and points necessary to help with 40 common conditions.

Lots of people are scared of needles, don't have an acupuncturist in town, can't get off work to go see one, or don't have the money. All these issues can be remedied by getting the full-color book and the included spring-loaded probe, ear seeds, and optional electric acupuncture pen. If you have ever been to physical therapy or a chiropractic office, you may have received a treatment where sticky pads were placed on your skin and muscles contract. The most basic term for this is a TENS unit.

The electric acupuncture pen is that same technology but packaged into a handheld unit with a small round tip. This e-pen allows a deeper and stronger stimulation (that you can control) to the points. You could also use cold laser but those units are quite expensive for home use (but just ask me and I can quote you a price).

What kind of conditions might you self treat? Anxiety, insomnia, back pain, headaches, numbness in their arms or legs, TMJ, upset stomach, asthma, and more. It isn't a cureall for everything; you still need to see your local doctor and make sure you're getting advice from someone local.

Acupuncture points and treatments can vary greatly depending on the school of thought you learned from as well as the doctor's experience. From my time interviewing acupuncturists on my podcast (A Doctor's Perspective), I didn't realize just how many techniques were out there.

This book is intended for you to do it yourself at home. Some points are located in hard to reach places like your back. Therefore, I dug deeper and found points on the ear that you can use to replace these. I include that ear acupuncture points pdf in the bundle order.

Everything is laid out with no history lessons or theory. This is just nuts and bolts blueprints and protocols of treatments. I have a quick reference list for you to see what conditions and points are needed. All the points are written out so you can find them without a medical degree, and pictures of each condition with each point are clearly shown.

I hope you enjoy this No Needle Acupuncture book and find the relief you have been hoping for. I would highly recommend upgrading to the electric acupuncture pen (epen) bundle pack so you get the fastest and best results. You can only get this on my website www.adoctorsperspective.net/bundlepacks and you can sample five conditions at www.adoctorsperspective.net/blueprints.

Doctors Save Your Marriage (2020-release date. Title may change)

This book is in the process of being written. It should be ready sometime in 2020 so if this interests you, check Amazon. I host a weekly podcast called A Doctor's Perspective where I interview other doctors about different aspects of practice: their specialty, marketing, goals, struggles, and staff. One thing I noticed from other podcasts I listen to is that many make lots of money and maybe have multiple clinics but in the process they get divorced. Usually, they lament what they could have done better and are disappointed they can't see their kids more often. Therefore for my show, I always asked the guests how to recharge with vacations and what can be done to keep the love alive in your family.

I combed through all those interviews and created topics and sub-topics of their best advice. This book will be a combination of lots of people's own experience on ways to structure your work, take time off, and actionable ideas to enhance relationships with spouses, significant others and children.

The book will be geared towards doctors of all specialties. Doctors have their own unique struggles with relationships and owning clinics and businesses brings special stresses. Being a business owner and a doctor increases your chance for divorce so if you aren't being proactive, bad things could happen. Therefore, implement some of the ideas in the book to maximize the relationships in your life.

Again, for the acupuncture, relationships, and health topics, I offer coaching. Call me or email me. I'd love to chat. You can get the help that you need, and I can be your coach, your guide, and encourage you to do the work. Make the learning curve quicker, save some time, save some money, and get out of your own way. I can help you in these areas and stop the self-sabotage. Don't give up too soon. Maybe all you really need is accountability. I'm here for you. So let's do this together. Let's make this year your best year yet. Email me: drtrosclair@gmail.com

Made in the USA
Monee, IL
14 September 2020

42359875R00042